SAINT PATRICK'S MISSIONARY JOURNEYS IN IRELAND:
THE SEVENTH-CENTURY ACCOUNTS BY MUIRCHÚ AND TIRECHÁN

By the same author:

Ulster & Its Future After the Troubles (1977)
Ulster & The German Solution (1978)
Ulster & The British Connection (1979)
Ulster & The Lords of the North (1980)
Ulster & The Middle Ages (1982)
Ulster & St Patrick (1984)
The Twilight Pagans (1990)
Enemy of England (1991)
The Great Siege (2002)
Ulster in the Age of Saint Comgall of Bangor (2004)
Ulster Blood (2005)
King William's Victory (2006)
Ulster Stock (2007)
Famine in the Land of Ulster (2008)
Pre-Christian Ulster (2009)
The Glens of Antrim (2010)
Ulster Women – A Short History (2010)
The Invasion of Ulster (2010)
Ulster in the Viking Age (2011)
Ulster in the Eighteenth Century (2011)
Ulster in the History of Ireland (2012)
Rathlin Island (2013)

SAINT PATRICK'S MISSIONARY JOURNEYS IN IRELAND –
THE SEVENTH-CENTURY ACCOUNTS BY MUIRCHÚ AND TIRECHÁN

Michael Sheane

ARTHUR H. STOCKWELL LTD
Torrs Park, Ilfracombe, Devon, EX34 8BA
Established 1898
www.ahstockwell.co.uk

British Library Cataloguing-in-Publication Data.
A catalogue record for this book is available
from the British Library.

ISBN 978-0-7223-4558-0
Printed in Great Britain by
Arthur H. Stockwell Ltd
Torrs Park   Ilfracombe
Devon EX34 8BA

CONTENTS

INTRODUCTION

A time chart of St Patrick's life in Ireland.

AD 385:   Birth of St Patrick in Scotland.

AD 401:   He is captured as a slave.

AD 407/8:   Enslavement at Slemish.

AD 408:   Escape back home.

AD 408/432:   He studies at Auxerre and Lerins in Europe.

AD 432:   The Pope sends Patrick back to Ireland as a missionary.

AD 432:   He founds a church at Saul.

AD 432/455:   He carries out most of his evangelizing.

AD 455:   He founds the Primatial see at Armagh.

AD 461/5:   Patrick dies and is buried at Downpatrick.

MUIRCHÚ'S ACCOUNT OF ST PATRICK'S MISSIONARY JOURNEYS

Two centuries had elapsed since the fifth century between St Patrick's death and the time when the professional historian Muirchú had started to collect source material for his biography of the Apostle of Ireland. Muirchú was the author of one of the two earliest accounts of Succat's (Patrick) death. However, it is not surprising to find in his works some confusion over names and places, and some details that cannot be reconciled with the *Confession*, the saint's devotional work and a declaration of faith. We must also take into account the inclusion of apocryphal material that had accumulated since Patrick's death in the late fifth century. But Muirchú's 'Life' of the saint emerges as an educational work by a sober historian, and he must be relied upon for more information about Succat's mission than St Patrick has given in his *Confession* and in his 'Letter to Coroticus', to the King of Ail in Scotland. Muirchú's sources were mainly based on information received from Aedh, Bishop of Sletty, who died in 699. It was Aedh that commissioned Muirchú to write Patrick's biography, and together they attended the synod convened by Adamnan in 695–7.

Muirchú would also have had access to the records of his own father or spiritual father Cogitosus, also a professional historian and author of the earliest known biography written about 650 of Patrick's disciple, St Brigid of Kildare. Both Bishop Aedh and Cogitosus may have in their youth conversed with people whose grandparents had lived when the saint was converting the Gaels or Milesians of the island of Ireland. They may have been party to a rich book of oral tradition.

As well as enquiries of the older historians and clerics, sifting through the oral tradition, Muirchú could obtain informative works that were chiefly of interest to academics. But it was useful, nevertheless, to know a little about them.

One text available to Muirchú was in the fifth-century 'Hymn of Secundinus' that praised Patrick's work and virtues. This is attributed to Sechnall or Secundinus, a fellow bishop of the Apostle of Ireland. It was written in the saint's lifetime. The hymn was written in the style of that early period made fashionable by Augustine's 'Psalm Against the Followers of Donatus'. It was in four line stanzas, each stanza beginning with a letter of the alphabet and in the popular Roman metre called verse quotations with fifteen syllables per line and a pause after the eighteenth syllable. The text of the hymn was written down after Muirchú's death; but in his lifetime, in the seventh century, the hymn was already a living tradition in both liturgy and popular belief.

Among the documents that may have been attributed to Muirchú was an earlier letter to Coroticus, mentioned by Patrick in his 'Letter to Coroticus' of which we do not have a text. There was also a letter known as to have been written down by Patrick to three Gaelic bishops, Cethiacus, Conall and Saceus, who had been conferred with holy orders without consulting the Apostle. Again Muirchú may have been able to make any reliable account based on the bishops, Patrick, Auxilius and Isernius. This was issued with the saint's express authorization about 450, between the date given for the death of Bishop Secundinus in 447 and that given for the death of Bishop Auxilius, in 459.

Muirchú was writing in the seventh century, but the later text of his biography of Patrick was of a later date. One in the *Book of Armagh* was dated to around the year 800; another was written in the eighth century and it is now in the National Library in Vienna, and it is thought to have been an eleventh-century manuscript in Brussels. But none of these texts were complete. The earliest complete text, a thirteenth-century work, showed considerable signs of rewording. In view of the unreliability of some of these original texts, we must follow the story of Patrick as told by Muirchú in the earlier manuscripts available.

Muirchú says that Patrick had arrived in the island, his ship full of religious treasures, at a place known as Coolenni or Cualann at a well-known port called 'Hostium Dee'. The harbour so described may be identified as Inver Dea, on the estuary of the River Vartry in County Wicklow, near Newrathsbridge, now called the Broad Lough. Upon landing, the saint decided that he should travel north to redeem himself legally from his old slave master, Lord Miliucc. If he expected his former master to still be alive, we must surely dismiss the possibility that the Apostle of Ireland at the time of his return to the island was anywhere near sixty years of age, and return to the assumption that he was nearly fifty. Patrick did not attempt a journey overland between Down and Slieve Mish (Slemish), from where he had escaped years before. He sailed along the coast, travelling northwards. He stopped first at Inishpatrick, a little grassy island a mile off the coast, opposite Maladide, a sea journey of about thirty miles which he could have covered between dawn and dusk. He passed the coast at County Louth, the mouth of Carlingford Lough, and the south shores of Ulster with the Mourne Mountains to his left; he finally sailed into a sound which Muirchú called 'Brene'. This must have been the strait between Killard Point and Ballyquintin Point, narrows that gave entrance to Strangford Lough. The rocks of Killard Point were named St Patrick's Rocks in memory of his route past them into the sound.

The missionary landed at the mouth of the Slane, hiding the boat there before going a short distance inland to rest. The river runs under a little bridge called Fiddler's Bridge on the Strangford–Downpatrick road, not far from the shore of the lough. The word 'Slan' from the Gaelic for health, refers to the health-giving properties attached to the Struell wells area.

A stone with two holes in it near the mouth of the Slaney has been cited by Father James O'Laverty as the spot where, local tradition has it, Patrick first prayed after landing in County Down. O'Laverty was the nineteenth-century author of the *History of Down and Connor*.

The saint and his missionaries were discovered in their hiding place, according to Muirchú's account, by a swineherd in the service of a man named Dichu. The swineherd, a pagan, good and natural, concluded that the strangers were a party of raiders. He fetched his master; it was Dichu's intent to kill the party, but as he looked on Patrick's face, God changed his feelings towards them. Now Patrick preached the faith to Dichu, who believed there and then, and the saint remained with him for some days.

Muirchú said that the place where Dichu found Patrick was the site, in his day, of a barn named after Patrick. This place was Saul, County Down, whose name derived from the Irish 'Sabhal', meaning barn. According to tradition Patrick founded his first church in Erin in Dichu's barn, on the site now stands a Protestant church, built in 1932, designed by Henry Seaver of Belfast in a style supposed to be that of an early Christian church, with a round tower. It was erected to commemorate the 1,500th anniversary of Patrick's arrival there as a missionary from Rome; it marked the place where he preached to his first convert. The fine windows of the church, depicting Patrick and his boat which he sailed into Strangford Lough, was by the Dublin artist Catherine O'Brien, a pioneer in stained glass work. Special services were held there on 17 March, Patrick's feast day. But it is also in regular use as the parish church for the local Church of Ireland community.

The present church at Saul replaced a plain, whitewashed building without tower or spire, built about 1770 on the site of a ruined abbey, which had suffered many attacks by the Vikings, and the plundering of

Edward Bruce in 1316. During this time Saul was an Augustinian priory, having been restored in the twelfth century by St Malachy for monks of that persuasion.

The Protestant community remembered the 1,500th anniversary of St Patrick's landing and the baptism of his first neophyte at Saul by the building of a new chapel. The Roman Catholic community commemorated the same event by erecting Stations of the Cross and an open altar on the slope of what would be called Slieve Patrick: a thirty-two foot high statue of the Apostle stood at the summit of the slieve. It is said that the sculptor fashioned Patrick's face on the head of the then Protestant primate of Ireland, Dr Arcy, Archbishop of Armagh. Bronze panels around the seat of the statue record scenes from Patrick's life. Each year, on the first Sunday of June, Mass is celebrated on the open-air altar.

Muirchú's account relates how the saint left his boat in the care of his proselyte Dichu. He now went north to Slemish, the scene of his six or seven years of slavery in the centre of County Antrim or the Kingdom of Dalriada. He wanted to accomplish his intentions of paying the price of his redemption from slavery to Miliucc, his former master. He hoped to win the King's esteem and to convert him. But Patrick may have been a good friend of Miliucc, who may have granted the young Patrick his freedom. As a Christian slave Patrick may have tried to convert the King. Miliucc, hearing of his return to Slieve Mish, had for some reason committed suicide.

Muirchú says that the proud old chieftain set fire to himself in his own dwelling together with his possessions. Patrick saw the charred remains of Miliucc's funeral pyre. He reached the south side of the slieve which was

14

marked in Muirchú's time with a cross. He looked over the place where he had been a slave. Hurt by the King's suicide, Patrick remained in silent meditation for about three hours. He wept and sighed. He said that none of Muirchú's sons or their descendants would ever succeed him in the kingship of his territory, but that they would be slaves for ever. He prayed and crossed himself, he quickly retraced his steps to Saul. He stayed for many days at Dichu's residence, going about on the entire plain, which he came to love, and to witness the flowering of the Church in the region.

The land around Saul has several places associated with St Patrick, but not actually mentioned by Muirchú. West of Downpatrick was Struell, where Patrick is said to have bathed. A church stood on the site for centuries, but the ruined, rectangular edifice now opposite the drinking well is a grassy hollow. It dates only from a rebuilding about 1750. The therapeutic qualities of the Saul waters are attributed to the blessing of St Patrick, and they are quite famous. The drinking well is a circular structure with a domed stone roof. The Eye Well, so named because its waters are reputed to cure eye disease, is a rectangular edifice with a pyramidal roof. Near to these wells are the bath houses, one for men and one for women. The water passes through two bath houses and then joins the main stream.

The night of 23 June and the Friday before Lammas are the special occasions for pilgrimage to the Struell wells. Writing in 1837 Samuel Lewis believed that on St John's Eve, the water rose in the wells as if by magic, and that the penitents and pilgrims made a circuit around the wells to pray, as a cure for serious and chronic eye diseases. A stone on the brow of the hill overlooking the well, known as St Patrick's Chair, or Patrick's Bed, was alone the centre of ritual circuits.

At Saul, Easter was near: Patrick's party discussed where they should celebrate it. By now the saint had learned that the most important of the Gaelic kings or *rís* was the High King, Loegaire, who had his stronghold in the Boyne Valley at Tara. Patrick travelled south, confident that he would drive the first wedge into the head of idolatry in the island.

It is thought that his strategy was to start at the top, by converting the High King, Loegaire, but the High King only held confederate powers so that it was not a foregone conclusion that the sub-kings would be converted, along with their 'subjects'.

Patrick and his missionary bid farewell to Dichu of Down. They did not attempt to travel across the mountains, or around them to reach the Boyne Valley. Patrick and his crew sailed out of Strangford Lough, heading down the coast into the harbour known to Muirchú as 'Inver Colpthi'. This was the mouth of the River Boyne at Drogheda, a distance of about fifty miles. They left their boat and went on foot until they reached the place described by Muirchú as the burial place of the men of Flacc. According to Muirchú, the place had been dug by slaves of the wizard Fechertni. Patrick pitched his tent and with his party, he prepared to celebrate Christmas.

The Boyne Valley is renowned for its prehistoric burial places – the mounds of Dowth, Knowth and Newgrange. Patrick had camped on a high hill at Slane, on the northern side of the Boyne, about twelve miles from the mouth of the river where he had left his boat. Presumably he had followed the northern bank of the river. Then he came along the southern base, they would have had to cross a dangerous ford at Slane in order to ascend the hill.

The Easter of Patrick's arrival, Muirchú says, coincided with an important pagan festival, celebrated with incantations, feats of magic and idolatrous rites, by wizards, sorcerers, soothsayers and experts in witchcraft. The High King was counted with kings, governors, princes and leading citizens. Muirchú likens the gathering to the court of ancient Babyon. One taboo associated with this pagan festival was that one might light a fire anywhere with the consent of the royal household.

On the hill of Slane, Patrick lit his paschal fire, and it was seen along the plain below, and as far as Loegaire's stronghold at Tara to the south-west. The High King called his elders and advisors and asked them, "Who dares to commit their terrible wickedness in my kingdom? Let him be put to death!" The elders and advisors were unable to name the culprit. The Druids told the High King that the offender's fire would not be extinguished that same night; it would never be put out, but it would surpass all the fires lit accordingly to their own custom. The King of those who lit the fire overpowered them all, and seduced the people: all powers should submit to it. King Loegaire's chief soothsayers, Lothroch and Lucetmael, predicted the arrival of a religion from across the sea: it would be proclaimed by a few and accepted by many. It would overthrow kingdoms, suppress monarchs who resented it, destroy the local gods, expel the wizards and would reign for ever. The soothsayers have been described as the men who would bring the religion. The

17

High King was deeply perturbed by the warnings of his wizards determined that the fire at Slane should not be extinguished, Loegaire decided to put an end to the matter by going to Slane at once to kill those who had perpetrated the sacrilegious act.

Chariots were yoked, twenty-seven altogether in accordance with pagan lore. The High King set out with his wizards with the most distinguished members of his court, to confront the offenders. On the way the wizards advised Loegaire to permit culprits brought to him to make obeisance rather by letting them go out to meet him. The Druids then proposed that they could compete with their adherents in the High King's presence, so that he could support them. Loegaire consented. When the parties reached the hill of Slane, they dismounted from their chariots and horses outside the enclosure where the paschal fire had been lit. Patrick was summoned to come outside to them. The wizards with Loegaire and his party did not stand when the saint arrived, and predicted that anyone who did so would become a follower of the new faith.

Patrick confronted the High King's party, singing in his heart verses from the psalms. One of his men, Ercc, not heeding the wizard's warnings, rose as the saint approached, and Patrick blessed him, and Ercc was converted.

A discussion ensued, in the course of which the wizard Lochru insulted the Church of Patrick. (Muirchú's account presupposes a little knowledge, at least, of Christianity in pre-Christian Ireland.) Patrick asked God to punish Lochru for his blasphemous words. At once Lochru was tossed up into the air and then dashed to the ground, head first, smashing his skull against a stone and dying before the eyes of the pagans, who were filled with fear.

Loegaire, enraged, ordered his men to seize Patrick and kill him, but the saint stood and cried out in a loud warning: "Let God scatter His enemies and let those who hate Him flee His sight." Darkness fell, and there was confusion among the pagans, who attacked one another in error. Now an earth tremor locked their chariots together and they went away, so that many were killed in the melee. Loegaire, his wife and six of his party, survived. His wife came to Patrick to ask and feigned conversion by genuflecting before him. It was planned to kill Patrick and his disciples, eight men and a boy, which was approved by the High King. Suddenly he was unable to see. Humiliated, the High King and his survivors returned to Tara.

The following day, Easter Sunday, Loegaire and his company discussed the events at Slane as they feasted in the banqueting hall of the royal fort at Tara. Patrick and his followers appeared in their midst. (Muirchú points out to his readers the analogy between this move and Church matters discussed behind closed doors.) One of the pagans rose to his feet, the poet Dubthach, who happened to be present. The saint blessed him and he became a believer. A young poet named Fiacc, who was staying with Dubthach, became a neophyte: he ended his days as the first Bishop of Sletty, the predecessor of that Aedh, Bishop of Sletty, who had commissioned Muirchú to write the 'Life of Patrick'.

Patrick accepted the pagans' invitation to their banquet. In front of others, Lucetmael poured some liquid from his goblet into Patrick's. The saint blessed his cup. All the contents were changed to a substance like ice, except for the drops that Lucetmael had added. Patrick poured these out, and blessed the goblet a second time, whereupon the contents returned to their first liquid state, to the disbelief of the gathering. Lucetmael now challenged Patrick to perfect signs and wonders, the first being to bring down snow on the land. Patrick replied that he refused to bring about what might be contrary to God's will. Lucetmael undertook magical spells, bringing down a fall of snow upon the land. He challenged Lucetmael to remove the snow, but the pagan replied that he could not do so before the next day. Patrick said to him that he could wreak evil but not good. He blessed the surrounding plain, and in an instant the snow vanished before the eyes of the amazed pagans.

Lucetmael invoked demons, and darkness fell. Patrick challenged him to lift it, but he was not able to do so. Patrick prayed and imparted a blessing. Light returned and shone before the court. Lucetmael believed that Patrick had a special power over water. Loegaire then suggested a test by fire; again Lucetmael protested, saying that Patrick had the power over fire and water. Patrick asked Lucetmael to wear his cloak, and one of Patrick's disciples, Benignus, should go forth into a hut, built half of green wood and half of dry wood. The house was hastily built. Lucetmael had gone into the part made of dry wood, before the assembled crowd, the hut was set on fire. Patrick prayed. The fire consumed Lucetmael and the green wood, leaving only Patrick's cloak untouched. Benignus, on the other hand, emerged unscathed from the dry wood, which did not burn. But Lucetmael's cloak which Benignus had been wearing was consumed in the flames.

Loegaire was infuriated. He rushed at Patrick, he would have killed him, had not God intervened. Patrick warned Loegaire that unless he believed, he would soon die, get struck down by the will of God. The High King, by now terrified, gathered his elders and advisors and told them that it would be better for him to live than to die. With their consent he accepted conversion the same day, as did many others. Patrick left the High King with a prophecy that he himself would live on to reign, because he had opposed him and sought to supress his mission, none of his descendants would ever succeed him.

Now setting out for Tara, Patrick pursued his mission – his preaching was confirmed by miracle signs.

Patrick was next back in Ulidia in confrontation with a man named Macuil whose rugged hilltop stronghold was in a place called Mocco-Echach, in what is now the barony of Iveagh. It was Macuil's custom to kill passing travellers. One day, Macuil saw Patrick walking peacefully near his stronghold and decided to kill him. He pointed out Patrick was the trickster who had misled many, and enjoined them to accompany him to test the power of Christ.

This they hoped to do by the trick of bringing to Patrick one of their number, who pretended to be ill. They brought the sick to Patrick and his disciples, and to ask for prayers to be heard.

The pagans did not like one of their company being ill, only now to find him dead. This miracle astonished Macuil's party, who realized the saint was truly a man of

God, and that he should not have him put to the test. The tyrant regretted what he had done, and submitted himself to Patrick's will, praising God as he proceeded. Macuil believed and confirmed his sins and was baptized. He asked of Patrick what punishment he merited for having intended to murder him. The saint told Macuil that not he, but God, would judge him. He instructed Macuil to set out for the seashore, partly clad, unarmed, taking none of his belongings and fasting at the coast. Macuil was to shackle his own ankle with fetters, throwing away the key and climbing into a small coracle without rudder nor oar. He relied on a wind to take him where he wanted, until he reached land where he was to live in exile and to obey the commands of God. Before Macuil left, Patrick raised to life the man who had pretended illness, so conquering death. Macuil reached the south coast where he fettered himself like a slave. He threw the keys into the sea and set sail in a boat which was driven by a north wind to the Isle of Man. There he founded missions.

Now Patrick found solace by fasting on the Sabbath by the sea, near the salt works that was on the northern side, not far from the 'Ox's Neck'; here Patrick saw some pagans working building a rath. He called for them not to work on the Sabbath, but they laughed at him. He told us that however hard they worked, it would be of no avail. Now a storm blew up in the night, and their fortification was washed away,

At Armagh, Patrick asked a wealthy landlord named Daire for a piece of land for a foundation, perhaps for a monastery. He requested a plot of high ground, willow ridge, but Daire told him that he would receive land on the lower ground. Muirchú tells us that in his time there was a martyr burning place near to Armagh. Patrick and his followers lived on the site until one day Daire sent a remarkable horse of his to graze in their meadow. This vexed Patrick, but Daire's groom ignored his complaint and left the horse there, only to find it dead when he returned next morning. When the groom reported that Patrick had killed the animal, his angry master ordered him to slay Patrick. But now Daire was struck dead. Daire's wife feared the progress of Patrick and his missionaries, sending two men to call the groom back, and to obtain Patrick's blessing, so that they would all be saved. The two emissaries said that Daire was ill. They wanted Patrick to send something to cure him. Patrick, knowing what had really occurred, blessed water and told him to sprinkle some on him and take what remained of it with him to them. The horse was brought back to life, as was Daire when the water was sprinkled over him.

Daire came to greet Patrick, bringing a gift, a bronze bowl. Patrick merely says that he exhorted his men to take the huge bowl back. The men came back to Daire and reported what had happened at which Daire again thanked him. He would have his bowl. He took it back to Patrick, and congratulated him on his firmness, and gave him the ridge that he had asked for, the site, says Muirchú, of the city of Armagh. Patrick and Daire climbed to the top to admire the view. They found a fawn at the top, where in Muirchú's time the altar of the Armagh churches had been placed. Patrick stopped him from killing the fawn which he carried about on his shoulders. The hind became as docile as a ewe and followed them, until Patrick freed the fawn in a place to the north of Armagh. The saint lay a curse on a field, that it would never be used by man or beast. The sea came up and the meadow became a salt mine to remain forever infertile.

Muirchú concludes his 'Life' (Vita) by recounting what he calls to be a few of Patrick's miracles, but he does not state where any of these events took place. A British princess Monesan moved by the Holy Spirit, was filled with great desire to know and serve the one true God. For this reason she was reluctant to marry despite her parents' insistence, but she continued adamant in her reluctance to marry. She urgently inquired about food. It would appear that the family were lapsed Christians, following the barbarous invasion of Britain, heathens of Christian extraction. The parents of Patrick had heard of his nearness to God, and they desired to give to Erin their daughter in the hope that he would enlighten her. After a long search they found her. Patrick heard Monesan's declaration of belief in Christ and baptized her with water and with the Holy Spirit, upon which she fell prostrate to the ground and gave up her spirit.

Muirchú tells us that in his day her relics were venerated in a nearby cave, in which they remained for twenty years after her death and burial, but he does not name the place.

A second miracle had occurred in the darkness – Patrick saw heavenly signs, and asked his believers, including Benignus, where they, too, perceived them. Benignus declared that he saw a divine vision – the Son of God and his angels revealed by the heavenly opening. Patrick said to Benignus that he had some success. The two went on to their usual place of prayer, where they kneeled in the river. When Benignus said that he could no longer endure the cold water, Patrick told him to step down from the place where he was to lower his position. There Benignus found the water so hot that it soon became unbearable and he had to clasp on to the banks.

The third and last miracle concerned Coroticus, the British chieftain to whom Patrick's letter was addressed. Patrick exhorted him to stop persecution and the slating of Christians, and to return to the way of truth. Patrick, however, learned that Coroticus had scoffed at his letter, whereupon he prayed to God to cast the traitor out from this world, and the next. Shortly after this, an important event took place where Coroticus heard a band of singers. Before his friend and the assembly of people, Coroticus took on the shape of a small fawn, and made off, never to be seen again.

On this note, let us turn to Muirchú's contemporary, Tirechán, who glorified the saint. Tirechán established a number of monastic foundations throughout Erin.

TIRECHÁN'S ACCOUNT OF ST PATRICK'S MISSIONARY JOURNEYS

Tirechán, the author of the other early account of Patrick's life, was a contemporary of Muirchú. He was a disciple of Ultán, Bishop of Ardbracan, County Meath. Tirechán had access to both the written and oral traditions concerning Patrick. Like Bishop Aedh of Sletty, Bishop Ultán, who died about 657, could have spoken with the grandparents in Patrick's lifetime. Tirechán seems to have written his memoir about 670, if we interpret his mission at the time of the plague of AD 664.

Tirechán's account must be approached with more caution than that of Muirchú. It had been written mainly in Meath and Connaught; it was concerned with the establishing of the extent of Patrick's foundation, and defining the *parochia* of St Patrick and the rights attached to it, a matter that had become a cause of concern by the second half of the seventh century.

If we read Tirechán more critically than Muirchú we should not relegate his account to the categories of the later purely legendary material. It should be remembered that a lot of what he wrote concerned seventh-century tradition of the saint's itinerary and exploits. Tirechán's account formed the basis for much of what had been handed down to become hallowed Patrick lore.

In Tirechán's account, as in Muirchú's, Patrick arrived as a missionary on the eastern coast of Ireland. He stopped at Inishpatrick and founded a church on the mainland, which was perhaps near Holmpatrick, and there he went by sea to the mouth of the River Delvin. Then he travelled into Meath, establishing churches in many places. At the Slane necropolis he ordained the Bishop Ciannán.

After the meeting with Loegaire at Tara, Patrick went to Teltown, an important place of assembly where archaeologists have confirmed literary accounts of pagan ceremonial festivals. The great festival of Lughnasen Aonach Tailteann took place there annually at the beginning of August.

From Meath, where the place named Donaghpatrick in Upper Kells barony commemorates a Patrician foundation, Patrick followed the Blackwater river westwards. He founded more churches at Derrypatrick and Assey, where there was an important Celtic assembly site at Uisneach in Ireland in ancient times. Here the Beltane festival was held on 1 May. The region was abundant in ring forts, carvings and enclosures of the Celtic era. From Uisneach, Patrick turned northwards through another barony in County Westmeath, to cross the River Inny into County Longford. Here he ordained the Bishop Mel, founded a chapel and also ordained Gosacht, a son of Miliucc where Patrick had served as a slave for six or seven years.

Tirechán offers no explanation here for the rather surprising introduction of Miliucc's son amongst Patrick's disciples but the possibility of other events was discussed later in this part.

Patrick's route now goes through County Longford, and over the plain called Mag Slecht that extended to the region of Bally Magauran in County Cavan, into County Leitrim crossing the River Shannon by the ford called the Two Birds, the pretty ancient stretch of the river in County Roscommon. At a plain named Duma Graid, Patrick ordained Ailbe to the priesthood. Duma Graid appears to correspond with the place near Doogary, found rather frequently in Connaght, there being six townlands of that name in County Mayo, and two in County Roscommon. Presumably the one referred to by Tirechán was the Doogary in Ballintober South barony, County Roscommon, a few miles to the north of the place where Patrick forded the River Shannon.

At Doogary, Patrick told Ailbe of a beautiful stone altar in the region, descendants of Ailill, from which it seems we may infer there was an earlier Christian settlement in the region, and some knowledge of the neighbourhood on Patrick's part.

Patrick's route continued northwards along the west bank of the River Shannon, to Moyglas in the barony of Ballintober North. Here he established another foundation which he left in the care of his monks. Still in East Roscommon, the saint received from the converted Druids the gift of his dwelling at Elphin. He left there in charge the Bishop Assicus, who was his goldsmith, with his nephew the Bishop Betheus, and his mother, Cipia.

From Elphin Patrick returned to Doogary and there

travelled out of the tuatha or tribal region, north again to Tawney in the barony of Tireveill, County Sligo. There accompanied him Mathona, a sister of Benignus. He founded a church which he left in the care of a brother named Cairellus.

From Tawney, the saint went north, retracing his route past Elphin to Rathcrogan near Tullisk at the well of Clebach beside Cruachan, he stopped. Rathcrogan is an ancient Celtic burial ground, rich in earthenware and ancient megalithic remains. The seven foot high standing stone in the centre of a ring fort is said to have marked the burial place of the pagan monarch Daithi. While Patrick and his followers were assembled at the well, two royal maidens came to wash their hands. Two daughters of Loegaire were being brought up in Connaught by two Druids or wizards, the brothers of Mael and Caplait. Surprised at the strange appearance of the monks and priests, the Irish asked who they were, and where they had come from. Patrick replied that it was better for them to believe in the one true God than to remain in doubt.

The girl asked – What is God? Where is God? Which is God? and Where is His dwelling place? The elders of the gods asked – Who is the Christian God? Is He immortal? Is He beautiful? Is He in heaven or on earth? In what way does He come to us, in the rivers or in the mountains or in the glens? Is He young or old? and In what manner is He seen?

Patrick was filled with the Holy Spirit, proclaiming that his God was the God of all men, the God of heaven and earth, of sea and river, of the sun and the moon and stars, of high mountains and steep valleys, the God of heaven; He has His dwelling place in heaven, and the sea. He rules over all things, He brings us to all things, He surprises everyone – He gives light to the sun by day and to the moon by night. He lords it over all dry land and has islands in the sea. He set the stars in their places. He is co-eternal with Himself, and in His own likeness. Neither is the Son younger than the Father, nor the Father older than the Son. The Father and the Son and the Holy Spirit cannot be divided.

As if with one voice and one heart, the two girls answered – all mankind should believe in the heavenly King. They wanted to believe and see His face. Patrick now assured them that in baptism the sins of their mothers and fathers would be accounted, to which they replied, "We believe." Patrick asked them if they believed in repentance after sin, in life after death, in the Resurrection, in the Day of Judgement and in the catholic nature of the Church of Rome. To all this the girls answered that they believed. They were then baptized, and Patrick blessed their white veils over their heads, and they begged to see the face of Christ. Patrick told them that they received the sacrament and feared death, they cannot see Christ's face, to which they replied – Give us the sacrament so that we may see the Son of God. They were wrapped together in one shroud, and they were mourned by their friends. The wizard, Caplait, the foster-father of one of the girls came to Patrick, lamenting. Patrick preached to him, and he also believed, and was tonsured. The other wizard, Caplait's brother, Mael, came to Patrick and told him that he would bring his brother back to his pagan ways. But the saint preached to Mael also, and he too was converted and tonsured. The period of mourning was nearly over, the bodies of Ethne and Fedelma were buried near the well of Clebach, a circular ditch was dug around the burial place as was customary, and Tirechán adds – "among the people of Ireland".

Patrick now founded a church named Shandonagh at Ard Licce, perhaps associated with Ardleckna, a townland in the parish of Aughrim in the same barony as Rathcrogan where the pagan princess and her tribe had been converted. Colman, a monk with deacon's orders, was left in that place.

At Ard Senlis Patrick left a woman disciple, Laloca, in the northern part of Ballintober South barony. He consecrated another site.

The saint now went with a bishop to his country. He passed on to Fuerty in County Roscommon, a few miles further south in another barony near the present border of County Galway, and in the tribal territory of Ui Maine. He placed a deacon in charge of this new foundation, leaving with him a book of baptism and perhaps a book of ritual. Patrick's followers separated from him here. At this place there were fifteen brothers, two of which were named as the Princes Bernicius and Hernicius, and a sister, Nitria. It was possible that these folk had come with the Apostle with Patrick's missionary expedition to Ireland, or had they joined his mission later? Tirechán, however, offers no explanation for their presence. These Franks continued to evangelize with success, founding churches in the territory of Castlerea, County Roscommon, or at a site Patrick indicated to them when they had come to him at Oran – in a barony which had been founded by Bishop Cethiacus.

Just south of Tulsk in the same country, at a place

called 'Duma Selce', Patrick blessed the Ui Briain, and remained for some time about a lake also called 'Selce'. Another church was founded and the Ui Briain baptized. Now he travelled further west, beside Lough Gara on the border of County Mayo, County Sligo and County Roscommon. He founded another church and blessed a well that never ran dry. Still in the neighbourhood of Lough Gara, Patrick's next church was established at Killaraght, named after Artachta – here he left a plate and chalice.

After an unhappy encounter with the son of Ercc who stole from him his home, Patrick reached the plain called Mag Airthig, which seems to have been to the west of Lough Gara in County Mayo. He stayed at Tullaghanrock a townland in Kilcolman parish. From here he travelled to Drummot Cerrigr to the south of Lough Gara. There Patrick came across two blood brothers fighting over the succession to their father's estate. He intervened and stopped their fight, telling them to be seated, and he made peace with them. For the sake of their father's soul, they gave land to the saint; on it he founded a church. He founded another chapel, a few miles further west, near the border of Clanmorris and Costello baronies in County Mayo, where he preached for a while. The next foundation was at Mucno's well, where in Tirechán's time a cross still marked the place where Secundinus had stood. From this site, Patrick travelled west to Connemara, to Kilmaine barony in County Mayo, where, according to Tirechán, he built a rectangular church. From this we may infer that the usual Patrick foundation was of the beehive sort of building.

Continuing his way northwards, Patrick stopped in the

barony of Carra, County Mayo. He founded a church and baptized many pagans. Travelling north-west, he came to Aghagower in the barony of Murrisk where Senach was ordained and made a bishop. Another church was established. The ruined church oratory and round tower at Aghagower perhaps stood on the site of Patrick's earlier foundation.

At length the saint reached the mountain with which he has been long associated – Croagh Patrick, the peak in the north of Murrisk barony, overlooking Clew Bay with its many islets. There was a good view from its summit, 2,500 feet above sea level. The view extends to the Twelve Pins of Connemara, to the mountains of Achill, and beyond Slieve League, to Donegal. Here Patrick spent forty days and forty nights in prayer, just like Jesus.

After his forty days on Croagh Patrick, he came down to found many churches in the barony of Murrisk and Burrishoole.

At this point the saint raised from his grave a swineherd, who had been slain by soldiers a century previously. The man was baptized.

We next find St Patrick among the people of the Ui Maine, where he founded churches in the forest of Foclut at Faragh, near Killala Bay; also at Murrisk, where now the picturesque ruin of a medieval Augustine friary stands. He journeyed eastwards through Tawney, County Sligo, once again to Aghanagh, also in Tirerill barony; the place was called Shanco. For the second time Patrick reached Drumlease, County Leitrim. Upon reaching the River Drowes, he blessed it to have an abundance of fish. Now he went east into the south of Donegal to a place called Mag Sereth in Turhugh barony, passing between Assaroe and the sea. Here he founded many more churches along the coast; there are small islands such as Inishmurray, now uninhabited, but rich in history, and here there is a ruined fort converted into a monastery in the sixth century, perhaps founded by St Molaise.

Patrick went on his mission to Inishowen, lying in Donegal, which is the north-west part of Ireland, where also pagan and early Christian monuments have survived. From Inishowen Patrick went into County Tyrone, where he ordained MacErc, Bishop of Ardstraw. There he crossed the River Bann to bless a site for a church in County Derry, and he founded other churches in that region. He proceeded on his way across the River Bush to reach Dunseverick, on the stormy coast of North Antrim, where the crag on which he sat was still known in Tirechán's time as 'Patrick's Rock'. The county is famous in the ancient legends of Ireland. Here was the landing place of Deirdre, a son of Uisneach, and along the coast, in the Sea of Moyle, the Children of Lir were turned into swans. In North Antrim he ordained Bishop Olcán, a disciple he had brought up from childhood, and left him with the relics of the Apostle Peter and Paul. The saint founded many churches in what is now the diocese of Connor.

The story brings Patrick to Slieve Mish or Slemish, where he was enslaved for six or seven years. He had looked after Gosacht, the son of Miliucc, and two of his daughters, and instructed them in the faith, and they feared the wizards. These children of Miliucc may have learned of Christianity from the young slave. They said that Patrick was a holy youth. This Gosacht was the disciple who was ordained by Patrick in County Longford. Perhaps Gosacht had addressed the faithful until the saint's return to the island, and they had become his followers. We must assume that Muirchú's account of Miliucc's suicide, and Patrick's prophecy that his descendants would all become slaves, is true.

Leaving Slemish, and the spot where he had seen the angel who told to him that a ship was ready for escape, Patrick passed into the territory of the Ui Tuirtri. Patrick baptized many in the barony of Cremorne, County Monaghan. He ordained one Victorus and founded a great church there.

After this circuit, Patrick founded another church for the priest, Justanus, attached to the community of Ardbraccan, County Meath, and he travelled into Leinster. He crossed the plain of the River Liffey, where he again established a church, and he ordained Auxilius and two others at Kilcullen, County Kildare. The present rambling village of Kilcullen lies about two miles from the remains of a medieval walled town built over an earth settlement. At Sletty, Patrick ordained Feccus the Fair and baptized the chieftain of Dunlainy. Continuing south through the Gowran Pass to Kells in County Kilkenny, he founded a church there, perhaps on the site of a large medieval priory on the edge of the village. He proceeded into Munster, where he baptized the sons of Natfraich. Additions by Tirechán to his account in the *Book of Armagh* tell us of a native Irishman, Iserninus, sent from France to Ireland as a missionary at the same time as Patrick. Contrary winds brought Iserninus to a landing place in the south of the island, where he reached his native territory. There he converted at least one of the family, preaching, baptizing and founding churches. His success provoked anger with the potentate Endae Cennsalach, with whom Iserninus and some of his followers had fled into exile.

After a while Patrick reached the potentate's fort at Rathvilly (The Fort of the Trees) in County Carlow. This fort can still be seen, its summit commands a good view to Lughnaquilla in the north-east, to mountains in Leinster in the south, and to as far away as Slieve Namon in the south-west and the Slieve Bloom range. The saint converted Crimthann, and obtained from him not only the freedom of the exiled Irishmen and his followers, but he also landed in Leinster. Patrick gave the land to Iserninus, who in turn gave it to his faithful neophyte. A religious community was now established at Aghade in the barony of Forth, County Carlow. There was also a convent near Aghade, established there by Dermot, King of Leinster, about 1151, perhaps on the site of the early Christian foundation.

Little was said of Patrick's death or burial. Tirechán relates that the saint lived to the age of 120, and that he was buried at Saul in County Down, where he had founded his first church in Ireland. It could be that he established a north-east church, as put forward by me in my book *Ulster & St Patrick* (Highfield Press 1984).

THE GROWTH OF LEGEND

The 'Triparite Life' and works was written in Irish about 895–901. It contains much lore about the saint, but a lot of it cannot be relied upon. In the 'Tripartite Life' we find that Patrick's place of birth was at Dumbarton in Scotland, a view put forward by the modern historian J. B. Bury. The first critical account of the saint was the work of the scholarly Protestant Primate of Ireland, James Ussher. For almost 200 years Ussher's account remained the only critical study of Patrick's life and the source of all information for Tirechán. Other seventeenth-century historians like Thomas Colgan relied on Ussher's work, as did Ballandus who also included a text from the *Confession* and the 'Letter to Coroticus'. In the 19th century there was a renewal of interest in the saint's life and legend. *Saint Patrick, Apostle of Ireland* by the Reverend James Heathrow Todd was published in 1864. The author was biased in his efforts to establish that Patrick was the true precursor of the established (Protestant) Church of Ireland. This led Roman Catholics to view his account as suspicious, Patrick's life was further examined by the uncritical works issuing from Roman Catholic authors. Other documents in the *Book of Armagh* were all original Irish texts of the 'Tripartite Life', published in 1887. By the twentieth century modern criticism of the saint had arrived, some saying that he did not exist at all. *The Life and Legend of Saint Patrick* was published in 1949, in which we can appreciate the figure of the saint as he was found in the realm of archaeology.

SELECT BIBLIOGRAPHY

A. B. E. Hood (editor), *St Patrick* (Phillimore).

Brian de Breffny, *In the Steps of St Patrick* (Thames & Hudson, 1982).

I. J. Herring, *History of Ireland* (W. H. Mullan & Sons, 1951).

James Carney, *Historical Memoirs of the Problem of St Patrick* (Dublin Institute of Advanced Studies, 1973).

James Stuart, *Historical Memoirs of the City of Armagh* (Brown & Nolan, 1900).

Maureen Donnelly, *St Patrick & the Downpatrick Area* (the author, 1995).

Michael Sheane, *Ulster & St Patrick* (Highfield Press, 1984).

P. W. Joyce, *A Concise History of Ireland* (The Educational Company of Ireland).